Other titles in the UWAP Poetry series (established 2016)

Our Lady of the Fence Post J. H. Crone
Border Security Bruce Dawe
Melbourne Journal Alan Loney
Star Struck David McCooey
Dark Convicts Judy Johnson
Rallying Quinn Eades
Flute of Milk Susan Fealy
A Personal History of Vision Luke Fischer
Snake Like Charms Amanda Joy
Charlie Twirl Alan Gould
Afloat in Light David Adès
Communists Like Us John Falzon
Hush Dominique Hecq
Preparations for Departure Nathanael O'Reilly
The Tiny Museums Carolyn Abbs
Chromatic Paul Munden
The Criminal Re-Register Ross Gibson
Fingertip of the Tongue Sarah Rice
Fume Phillip Hall
The Flaw in the Pattern Rachael Mead
The Sky Runs Right Through Us Reneé Pettitt-Schipp
Walking with Camels Leni Shilton
Wildlife of Berlin Philip Neilsen
Aboriginal Country Lisa Bellear
Moonlight on Oleander Paul Hetherington
Broken Ground Steve Armstrong
Satan Repentant Michael Aiken
Open Door John Kinsella
Poor Man's Coat Christopher (Kit) Kelen
Stone Mother Tongue Annamaria Weldon
Legacy Julie Watts
Keeper of the Ritual Shey Marque
The short story of you and I Richard James Allen
Autobiochemistry Tricia Dearborn
The little book of sunlight and maggots Michael Aiken

Previous books by Michelle Cahill

The Accidental Cage (Interactive Press, Brisbane, 2006)
Ophelia in Harlem (Kilmog Press, NZ, 2010) chapbook
Vishvarūpa (Five Islands Press, Melbourne, 2011, reprinted 2012)
Night Birds (Vagabond, Sydney, 2012) chapbook
The Herring Lass (Arc, UK, 2016)
Letter to Pessoa (Giramondo, Sydney, 2016) short stories

Books edited

Poetry Without Borders (Picaro, 2008)
Contemporary Asian Australian Poets edited by Boey, Aitken and Cahill (Puncher and Wattmann, 2013)
deciBels series 3 (ten chapbooks, series editor, Vagabond, 2018)

Michelle Cahill's poetry thrives on cultural crossings, assembling the materials necessary to sustain an identity in multiple settings. The result is a poetry of observation in which the subject position, and so the way of seeing, is always in flux. We have no reason to suppose that the speaker of any given poem is the poet. Nothing is taken for granted, and anything might serve the purpose of explanation; this is poetry seeking constantly to find a place in the world. The lasting impression is of a language made beautifully specific, where the specifics in any given poem serve to construct, not simply reflect, the speaker's environment.

David Herd

From the exploration of love myths to the celebration of Mumbai, from an extraordinary portrait poem like 'Sīta' to the humorous eroticism of 'Pārvatī in Darlinghurst', the poems in *Vishvarūpa* show a breadth of human understanding and unassuming wisdom that matches their extraordinary verbal flair. With rich intoxications and buried longings, Cahill, in the best tradition of poetry, expands our sense of who we are.

Peter Boyle

Michelle Cahill spans the distance between myth and reality, Australia and India with an ardent intelligence. In beautifully polished, elegant language these poems romp and sing, and they also surprise with moments of subtle tenderness. This is a strong, disciplined, uncompromising poet who delivers probing and deeply engaging work.

Judith Beveridge

From its dreamlike opening poem 'Something Like a Reverie' Cahill's luminous collection of poems about India and Australia opens up its own reverie that is rich, insistent and full of lush sensory detail. The poetry's naturalistic, often story-like style is unassuming, yet executed with great precision and discipline. Transporting the reader from Darlinghurst to Mumbai, from garden to temple, these poems resonate with the author's clear-eyed wonder, quiet, precise powers of observation and gleaming turn of phrase. In a long list full of technically brilliant poets working at full stretch, Michelle Cahill's *Vishvarūpa* was a quiet, poised delight.

Judges Report, 2012 Victorian Premier's Literary Awards

Vishvarūpa

Michelle Cahill

Michelle Cahill writes fiction and poetry. Her short stories, *Letter to Pessoa*, received the UTS Glenda Adams Award, the NSW Premier's Literary Award for New Writing and was shortlisted in the Steele Rudd Queensland Literary Awards. She won the Hilary Mantel International Short Story Prize and was shortlisted in the ABR Elizabeth Jolley Prize. She was a Fellow at Kingston Writing School, a Visiting Scholar in Creative Writing at UNC, Charlotte, and a Fellow at Hawthornden Castle. She is an award-winning poet and critic. Her essays have appeared in the *Sydney Review of Books*, *Southerly*, *Westerly* and *The Weekend Australian*. Michelle is the founding co-editor of *Mascara Literary Review.*

Michelle Cahill

Vishvarūpa

Published in 2019 by
UWA Publishing
Crawley, Western Australia 6009
www.uwap.uwa.edu.au

UWAP is an imprint of UWA Publishing,
a division of The University of Western Australia

ISBN: 978-1-76080-035-2

First published by Five Islands Press, Melbourne, in 2011.

A catalogue record for this book is available from the National Library of Australia

Inside front cover image: 'Anatomy of Stillness' by Clare Arni, Andra Pradesh, 2013
Designed by Becky Chilcott, Chil3
Typeset in Lyon Text by Lasertype
Printed by McPherson's Printing Group

This project has been assisted by the Australian Government through the Australia Council, its arts funding and advisory body.

for mum and dad

The tortoise can draw in his legs
The seer can draw in his senses
I call him illumined

Bhagavad Gīta
(translated by Swami Prabhavananda
and Christopher Isherwood)

Contents

Something Like a Reverie

It happens that you wake before dawn,
dreaming you walk the empty streets
as unfinished threads of rain stitch their
needlepoints. Your bare feet stumble
over fruit, half-eaten, clipped from trees
where sulphur-crested cockatoos hang,
conspicuous as bleached handkerchiefs.
Their strange cry bids you to wander
after dogs tire of barking or your lover
stirs closer with his inordinate devotion.

You see beyond the drapes of windows
into Federation homes, observe the messy
tangle of arms, bed sheets, legs and hair.
Turning then, to follow the scent of those
imagined flowers, their colours masked
by a darkness which is deeper, softer
even, than everything you've buried.
You know the day brings nothing eventful.
Cut lunches, shoelaces, ironed uniforms.
How during school hours the roof creaks,
the lizards escape your tread to and from
the clothesline. How the garden's beauty
defies all reason, being pointless as ever.

The Abbey

Why do you ask? Haven't we already touched
as we lay on the lichen, the stones, uneven and
tessellated into a path, your hand on my dress.

We lay with forget-me-nots, whispered vows
resting our gaze. The air was heavy as the scent
of lilies stewed and spilt across the dry grass.

I felt the shock when you parted my hair.
I saw crushed petals falling from the sky
like paper moons in flawless pink and red.

I believe there was a dead dove, its neck swollen
as if it had been strangled. And I saw what looked
like one stagger into the shade of a fluted yew.

We could hear the voices of those we knew,
the organ player's notes receding from the abbey,
the sound of wooden bells. Or was it broken wings?

Impossible to read the names. How could we see
the living or the dead ghosts rise from their graves,
pacing, becoming frantic. Our eyes were stitched.

All that we saw was the soil, sweet and sad, leaves
beginning to fray, to curl, and the splatter of moss
sown like a seam through stone, a silent threnody,

a trickle beneath the earth's skin as if something
stirred in darkness that was unspoken, the dove's
wings, perhaps, or the heart weighing its secret.

The Ghost-Ship

I found the man alone, rocking in a ship's hull,
off the island, the winds baffling, a lee current
lifting anchor, purling rain on the grey horizon.

There was an albatross in the cradle of his elbow;
the bird slain. The scent of cold feathers, a musk
pungent as magnolia, tossed with brine and bilge.

Outside, the moon glimmered in haloes. The ship
was ghost-like, abandoned by its crew, and the eye
of the albatross was a dark crescent, strangely wide.

Waves slapped against the ship's bow as it creaked,
testing the ice floes. Storm petrels cried and faltered.
Perhaps the only other sound was the man's breath.

I lulled him to sleep. I rowed him ashore in a dinghy.
His body heavy as words I could not speak and slight
as a fledgling's neck. Snow fell thickly where we lay.

But it was hardly a man's form I touched, more
like an iris, purple veined, and intricate. I might have
milked the sepals for nectar or swallowed his dreams.

I might have promised him lovely things; perhaps
an ice-petrel's wing, a green, glassy wave, a few beads
of amber as daylight broke and he rose from sleep.

The moon had crept away from the shore into oblivion.
The man was deafened, so he said, by whale song,
a warble, loud as the chaos of a children's playground.

Take me home to the ghost-ship, he implored, with politeness
and cowed rage, and the moment he uttered these words
I saw the vessel pitching in the storm, in colossal waves.

Soon the man was in his cabin, still spellbound by the song
of lost leviathans, the smell of brine, bilge, and burning oil.
Birds circled the grey skies, but there was no white albatross.

And now, when I look from the shore, I see no ghost-ship
for the snow is falling like a bitter hymn. Sometimes, I think
I see the baleen whales spout a fine spray, as they rise, sighing.

The Chase

Yesterday's clouds leavened the autumn sky as we walked
along the muddy trail by the creek, to where the rains flowed,
spilling over the scent of soil, the secrets of moss-covered stones.

We passed the tannin bay, still and cold with its floating negative,
a silhouette of ridge where the needles and tips of the tallest,
oldest trees were streaked by light or by the wind's vibrations.

Silt crabs burrowed the mangrove swamp, trapping plankton.
Twisted angophoras led to a summit where speckled rocks
invited the khaki song of cicadas to smooth out every pause.

And trekkers came, their voices strident over the music of rain
as it splashed from sandstone middens and cantilevers, and we
had to stop right there to wait for calm. The rain left its stain

on those cliffs – deep and tawny as it filtered, threading down
to where we stood. I wondered what was left – broken shells
frail wings, fins, the bones and minerals of the Gadigal,

their tribes wiped out by smallpox over two hundred years back.
We were shaded there by water-gums and lilly-pilly, as we
weaved through the darkness, the lavender scent of evening

which is a drug. It drives you to the periphery, the deepest part
of this gorge where at last we crossed the river, our feet cold
amongst the tangled roots and the rain. We stayed, until

we could no longer bear the sound of the waterfall drowning out
the cicada's song, a lyrebird's retreat in the moonlight – this
partita where water, light and leaf are blurred into one green.

Deva Loka

The road leads us away from the temple of Pārvatī,
from the iris of the spotted hawk, red and gold satin,
the smoke of burning *dhoop* and coconut offerings.
Away from bells touched by the fingers of pilgrims.
As we wind across the range down steep hairpin bends,
we are losing our *mukti*, already forgetting what we have left;
the *deva loka*. The red dirt crumbling beneath our sandals
was the undoing of *nāmarūpa*, a reminder of Shiva's hip
thrust in *tribhanga* against the gravity of this place.
Beyond us, the peaks of Trisul, Kamet and Nanda Devi,
the Gharwal Himalayas, binding like a white turban
wave after wave of denuded hills and barren ramparts.
Blood-coloured as a lotus, the sun descends, setting
alight the candles of juniper, *sal* and *bhojpatra*,
the sky's oxides, the dust of Dehradun.
Each bend in the road is a new discovery, an act of faith.
We glue our gaze to what lies ahead: a crossing of cattle,
donkeys weary from the day's toil, goats feeding on riverine scrub,
children playing cricket, the maids and *gopis* of some myth
or *chanda* collecting fuel and water, the road workers,
constructionists and wielders, dressed in thongs and scarves,
carrying their hoes, spades, sieves.
Soon we'll be back in the town with its car horns, its tinkle
of cycles and rickshaws, its smells of oilcake and cardamom.
We'll return to the house as vendors close their stalls,
as monkeys loping from a telegraph wire cast shadows
as a street-sweeper burns his rubbish for warmth.

Ode to Mumbai

for Dilip Chitre, after his 'Ode to Bombay'

Piece by piece I'll remove your unwieldy syntax.
I'll taste your jaggery, as the street's kaleidoscope
triggers a new explosion. I'll tear up draft after draft,

while you scorn my attempts to write an elegy
or an epic. Not your first beggar or *bailadeira*, I, too,
am engendered, colliding with *hijras* who float like dark

moths weaving through Santa Cruz traffic. I'll find
relief in each disappearance and hallucination, discover
your tableau of devas, slumdogs, spivs and impresarios

is a divine smokescreen or a hologram that easily bends
into a new simile. But when held up to the light
I'm left with only negatives. Mumbai, even your name

is a philologer's conundrum, as mine is the antithesis
of my self, a colonial slip. Strip the layers, what remains
are the bones, a different grammar for equivalent parts

of speech, the same ivory teeth in any caste or creed. I
hang in a gap between the sound and meaning of words,
dipping my subconscious in different time zones, where

my bed is a temple and a brothel, where dream defines me.
Your poem has a history, in which my pages are missing.
I rise from the poem on a burning ladder of language.

Prayerflags from Dharamsala

Dussehra

I am dancing tonight in the Kangra valley.
Thorn bush and effigies of the demon king
Ravan are ablaze, flickering for Dussehra.

Karma, Lobsang and Abhishek are quietly
drunk. A smell of wood mingles with grass,
gasoline and sweet clove; the crowd is delirious.

Night's skin is adorned with chariots, palanquins
and fizzed with firecrackers. But in Temple Road,
Macleod Ganj, an image of Hu Jintao is doused

in petrol, incinerated by Tibetan protesters.
I take photographs with the Reuters journalist,
who is charming, who thinks this is all a joke.

Rangzen

The activist Tsundue, who wears a red scarf
is the man I've come to meet at Rangzen ashram,
in the shadow of Gorijnda, Pārvatī's mountain.

He speaks of human bones on the steppes to Tibet,
escape routes, border towns where he was detained,
house arrests, months before the Bejing Olympics.

My fingers caress a cigarette. I watch censored
documentaries, a film by Dhondup Wangchen,
imprisoned in Lhasa with twelve hundred missing.

And Philippe, whose book records the resistance
to Chinese mining is counting on the Dalai Lama's
editorial being sufficient to sway the neo-liberals.

We drink whiskey, we huddle in coats as the sun
lingers before it sinks below the Dhauladhur spur.
My memory card is blank, my photographs lost

but there are voices in the darkness, eyes without
faces: Acha, Nyingje, Lobsang, Hip Hop, Army.
Émigrés, mostly, we are harried by quotidian gods.

Dusk covers our bones in tumuli. Wind brakes
the nocturnal trees, our motorbikes swerve as
we drive to the edge of the steep, sliding road.

Nasreen

The moon spills her mettle through the pines,
silhouetted conifers scrape the night sky,
the guesthouse cloaked as I stumble home.

My instinct fails and I take a wrong turn,
climbing the scrub-ravine by torchlight.
The men in the village are dizzy with joy.

My room is just the same, walls screaming
in silence. I turn on my laptop, fiddle with lines
about death as revelries rise from the valley.

Nasreen serves chai and sweet rice. He is tipsy.
We talk in a nervous patois of English-Hindi,
in a voice that retreats from its subject before

it can ever be defined. I begin my endless
revisions, to modify clauses, edit adjectives
until my hands are too numb to type. I smoke.

Count falling stars. From the balcony I watch
the vapour of breath vanish, the cigarette's
ember in the pin-cold night. Perhaps for solace

I charge my phone. Sleep in a throw of blankets,
the room dusty, with peeling paint, a broken
window, and a shy spider, the size of my hand.

Lung-Ta

If I drift towards the space between now
and my own Shangri-La, the shadows
have names. They speak another language.

At breakfast I watch the glistening
wingspan of a koel curve through the forest,
The pines disguise their idiom of crows.

I feed cake crumbs to the pied finches
who enter my room, leave the crumbs
untouched and fly away with precision.

School children climb the hill to Dharamkot.
Gypsy donkeys decked with bells and bags
of cement shamble to a new construction site.

All day the scoop of shovels. Lean women
toil to feed their children. I scrawl a few lines,
the incense burning into broken strings of ash.

Fakir

Maybe this is a story about the photographs
of Tsundue, Rangzen, Dussehra, each touristic
moment gone. Maybe it's about the word *freedom*.

Or maybe it's about the eyes without faces,
the ones that stay open, refusing to dream
when lips are sewn by moonlight's threads.

Prayer flags float over the drunken town.
A child cries in the valley. A blind beggar crosses
the noisy chaos of the street, with its hawkers

and cycle rickshaws as boys rev their motorbikes
past Guru Nanak's store. I pursue him with an urge
to taste the darkness he walks, which feeds him.

Six Myths of Love

Psyche

Carried on the wings of Zephyrus, waiting
in an empty warehouse from where I view
the city's clock towers and cathedral spires.
I watch bats knit the dissolving winter sky.

Dusk brings you close enough for me to trace
the broken lines in your hands. There are maps
uncharted, swithering currents. There is no
language other than now. Like candle or snow

you disappear, leaving what is undisclosed.
While trains keep time, and streetlights burn
you draw me from midnight's cusp. Birds rise
from your hands into the bleeding shadows.

Agape

My tutor in anatomy was an American research student with a slit in his heart like a mailing box. It was dark inside that wound. You couldn't see inside but you could easily post messages. For months I sent him hand-written notes and he turned them into roses. Red, pink, mauve, hybrid-blue, black. Their scent drowned out the acrid smell of formalin. They bloomed in my basin, my bed and in the pages of my textbooks. Haunted by the heart's diction, I grew to love polysyllables like *myocardium*, *papillary*, *tricuspid*. I composed my own acronyms. One day the slit in his heart was sutured neatly. My tutor's appearance became woody like a fruit tree that stops flowering. He changed his name to a hyphenated form and we spoke a different language now. It was winter on campus and fortunately I came to be taught in Latin by an eccentric Professor of Anatomy. So it was back to the dictionary, back to cadavers and back to the bones. I learnt to tolerate the acrid smell of formalin. I learnt that pig heart is reasonably similar to human heart, making porcine tissue ideal for transplantation, and running little risk of rejection if treated with serial dilutions of glutaraldehyde. It was a source of great comfort for me to discover that we are akin to other species, in matters of suffering.

Narcissus

The word became flesh.
And we shacked up together.
No bigger than a flash-drive,
my cyber soul
likes to speed-date.
I am this text. I reply
obediently, ardently
fed by a circular flow
through carotid arteries,
veins, fingertips that pause
to scroll and submit
are quick to delete.
Each truth a synapse.
Each glyph a pulse.
A palindrome.
Language encrusted
in its armature,
a thick patina.
We talk all night.
We talk about the body.

Asclepios

To dissect a living heart you need a bloodless field
a heart-lung bypass. You need to stop the heart
from beating to find the blockage you wish to remove.
Guided by a knowledge of the precise location
between the second and sixth ribs, left of your incision.
Note colour, shape, size, weight, presence of clots,
presence of disease, you observe external linings,
ventricles. You watch perfusion, harvest the graft.
Suture it like a ribbon across the knot. How easily
the tissues separate in a plane beneath your scalpel
without resistance, despite scars and calcified plaques.
There are layers, territories beyond evidence or image,
a surgeon's casebook of anomalies waiting to be signed.

Aphrodite

Pick up my pieces – I was born
of foam, shell, my tongue sweet
and salty, the sea my etymology.

To distract the minds of men or
gods, I loosen my skirt. Prized
for what I do not say. And how.

Who could blame me for being
stuck on myself? Seductive, yes.
Surely, if irretrievably mistaken.

Adonis, I'll purchase you again.
Hunter of stags and hare, reeking
of slaughter, I'll match your sport.

Make of your blood and nectar
a pomegranate, whose blossoms
the wind weaves and breathes.

Eros

What a cliché you are. With such
élan, strutting about at the bar.
Though imperfection is desirable.

Show me your wit, your weapons,
your leaden tip or golden arrow.
For I have never known such praise.

I write your name in my sleep,
I turn your hand, a fallen leaf.
Now, there is no fear of death,

I've broken my promise. Sirens,
burning oil spilled on your shirt,
lipstick smudged all the way down.

I am exiled, somewhere between
my old and my new skin, in liminal
hours when waking is a dream.

Childhood

The afternoon cruises,
after badminton, lemonade
and chutney sandwiches.
Voices are like ribbon made
for unwrapping the past.
Syllables of imaginary laughter
blend with the real, as I recall
the warmth of uncles, aunts, cousins
left behind in foreign cities,
Mumbai, London, Goa.
I think of the bright day when dad
flew our kite on Primrose Hill.
It's hard to say what matters.
Everything fragments,
defers to time's calibrations,
the long shadows are deceptive.

I piggy-back my daughter
in summer's leaf-light.
We swim laps in tandem
riding a pink foam noodle, sinking fast,
her tiny arms a choker for my neck.
I'm weak to her commands, her tears.
In any competition, I must lose.
The dragonfly's flight is a tease
never kissing its reflection,
a cross-stitch lacing the pool.
The distant hum of the freeway
sounds like a hole in the heart,
the softest turbulence.
The garden is a green humidicrib.

In My Father's Absence

Word charms, my dandelion head
pistilled with those sweet nothings.
It was always from her that I borrowed,
so eager to believe the sliding vowels.
Mother pumped the swing's far reach.
I soared above park benches, the day's
insults. She-oak and leaf litter beneath
my feet were fractions, indulging
a love of detail, of composition, which
extracts the perfume from such scenes.
The context hinged on a southerly,
a painted boatshed, vying for light,
the catamarans aligned and gridlike.
Pelicans kneeled like nuns, their water
liturgy became the lake's salt hum.
I pretended to ignore my mother's
post-coital hush, her sleep abandon,
how his hand broke her weave,
how he prised her reluctant mouth.

Near us a boy with cerebral palsy
groaned in incoherent prayer.
His grimace like the spiritual angst
of some aberrant-winged angel.
I saw there in his guardian's blank
features, a monotone of suffering
for the way love tolerates. Mother,
with her man in my father's absence:
how tireless she was, how fatigued.

(In)Visible

Lines erased, less than
form. No breath or shiver
stirs my doppelgänger. This void
of corridors leads nowhere, though
I can hear the sound of doors opening, closing.
Smiles fall away to unease.
The light concentrated, refracted by
so small an aperture, becomes brilliant,
losing its object to radiance.
There are discourses of the spectral,
the numinous in which, it seems,
I exist in parentheses.
Tears and sweat accessorised.
My body, sensual, without culture
bears no initial.
My home,
colonised by language.
(Yours).

There are those who admire the geometry,
these metaphors of space.
Be elevated, they advise. Take in the air,
the uncommon with the requisite.
What is ethics? Not smugness
or complacency. Not prescription.
Nothing which is not political.

City of Another Home

City of seven islands, guarded by eight-armed Mumbadevi,
of the Dravidians, Marathis and Gujaratis, your name
alludes to the Portuguese word *bahia*, meaning a fine bay.

City of slum redevelopments and Arabian Sea penthouses,
the homes of divas, impresarios, fashionistas. City of hedge
funds and investments you teach me to forget the present *jīva*.

City of muddy shores strewn with litter like tissues clinging
to the naked mangroves, I'll wander your streets that smell
of *pomfret*, *kolambi*, dried dog faeces and Bombay duck.

City of rags, overflowing drains, sacred graffiti, I'll lose myself
in bazaars where the Koli women haggle sharply. I'll step out
to cross an anarchy of traffic like Aravanan guided by Krishna.

City of taxis tagged by freewheeling touts selling copies of copies,
I'll pity your beggars who drift into wanderlust and blockbuster
deliriums on a road that belches dust clouds, bitumen, gravel.

City of spivs, sadhus, acronyms and dual-use accents, I'll miss
your ennui after the Colaba hostage scenario, after a river
of blood washed the platforms of Chatrapati Shivaji station.

The pundits pronounce blanket claims against the slogans
of democracy. The victimised moan about Moguls, mobs
jihadists, anti-Zionists, Al-Qaeda but I come home to Mumbai.

Today, I've woven your hybrid threads into a present warp.
Walked past Anglican churches, gardens splashed in hydrangea,
jacaranda, agapanthus. Empty of composure, inside out,

I drift from gardenia-scented evenings to ante meridiem,
half-aware that it's ineffable to love a city that was never
really my home, or a home whose walls are flaky as paratha.

Fathomless to sleep in rooms watched over by the Virgin Mary,
by saintly relics and faded portraits of deceased relatives.
To endure dogs howling beneath jackfruit trees, a dark *raga*

lingering in the nightmares of chary spinster aunts. To find
in this quiet enclave of *gymkhanas*, terrace parties and convent
schools that dawn breaks tenderly, a half-remembered prayer.

City of nostalgia, I'll miss buttercups, halwa, holidays in Goa.
City of dubious promises your people feed crows by the freeway.
In the smear of sunset's human river, your pilgrims make *pūjā*,

buying and selling divine paraphernalia. Time is measured by
the metronome of a bullock's tail, by night's amphetamines.
I'll sit on the steps with David, Sharlene and Lima; get stoned

on home-grown as the ceiling fan unsticks the liminal moments,
as tradesmen render another curtain of cement over the walls
of a shaded, crumbling bungalow I can't yet abandon to memory.

City of divine deliriums, the dogs are chained. The Laughter Club
members fatigue their raucous morning bellows from a plinth
of recreational park. The auto-rickshaw *wallahs* doze in the shade.

Sīta

She came from the *chawls* of Kamathipura,
those ancient five-storey houses with their long *varandas*
swanned by ladies of the night, who leant over banisters,
whispering in dark alleys, wearing rouge and *kajal*.
Keeper of beds, cheaper than *kothi* for public servants,
for drunken men of the village,
more outcast than *dalit*, *bhangi* or *dhobi*.
She came from the *chawls* of Karnatipura,
jangling her ankle bells, with deep-throated taunts
prodding me on the train to Andheri when I was a foreigner
in my own country. I was ten years old
on summer vacation, packed in the Ladies carriage,
dressed in t-shirt and Levis, among the garlands, the *ghagras*;
ingenuous to her chicanery, her occult skill;
not knowing beneath her sari the unspeakable scars
of custom and ridicule. A cultural fragment out of context,
a gender beyond my Christian judgements, fata morgana,
a ficto-critical anecdote. I'd never read the epic myths
or studied Sanskrit. I was ignorant of Lord Krishna
made incarnate as the beautiful Mohini and engaged
to Aravanan. Her name was Sīta, once from Bihar.
She was beaten and disowned by her family, assaulted
by beggars, by police; a harridan, an anarchist, her blouse loose
and gaudy, her eyes so wild I would not forget.
She came from the *chawls* of Karnatipura, a bathhouse,
where she lived with her mothers, her sisters and her friends.

Hanumān

A monkey swallows the sun, unpeeled fruit of the sacred river.
I've crossed two oceans, ferried through the straits of Malacca.
I've been swept in currents of borrowed language to the steps

of this ghat offering my *pūjā* of *pushpa, chandan, deepak, dhoop*;
awake to the clamour of death, the drips and splashes of water,
awake to the sound of sitars, temple bells and Shiva's conches.

It's too early for Bhangra, in Benares the sons of merchants
breathe the slumber of *paan*. A crow waits in the mango tree
as the pigeon trainer scatters grain, paying homage to the dawn.

The river is flotsam, forgetting her deities, shedding her scales.
Soon, in the breeze, kites will rise and plummet with the ash
of burning flesh. I too am a kite, the strings of my words tangle.

Hanumān, it is said the shadow of a god measures thirty *yojanas*.
You overcome calamities the size of mountains. Your shadow
slips between temples, an alter-ego moving between two worlds.

Shaping the Linga

Under the intent of his mineral gaze lies a tripwire,
        and a girl who shies from bright,
bangled wives. She follows him through Panjim,
                its burnt yellow facades,
past chapels, basilicas, famous relics, ramshackle bars.

They take a lane to her grandfather's whitewashed house,
        the heat lingers like a scent and it is beautiful
to enter the bare room with its wooden crucifix,
                as the light unspools
and flutters in rosettes across a stiffly plastered ceiling.

To stray in the fragrant flower gardens, shaded by laburnum,
        by the mango tree, and *caju* tree, as evening breaks,
and the koel flits from leaf to leaf, and the thrush sings
                a foreign, plaintive song.
A song nameless to the heart, that can't quite be forgotten.

For there are plenty of ruins, crimes. Temples were denied
        their *mahadevas* and *kalavants*. At Sri Mangeshi
they taxi to a shrine desecrated in the years of Inquisition.
                Girls curve their fingers
in cow dung, butter, in sandalwood, shaping the Shivalinga

with such devotion, as if they are losing themselves to a god,
        as if there's no need for translation,
for a language they are yet to learn.
                The moon in her tabernacle
bears witness to the forced conversions of a crumbling city.

Now the girl is fourteen or sixteen, possibly; hard to say.
She slumps against his motorbike, chatting, smiling
before they race the fine sands of Calangute.
Women raise the hems of saris,
dip their ankles in foamy seas, the moon, a transparent host.

He would save her from hippies, from wild rave parties
as they leave the beach, blasting with trance
and he finds his adversary in Shiva,
the boatman, the rapper,
whose twist of arms and dreadlocks bid her to boldness.

She can barely sleep in the village with its insect-nights.
Out there – a maze of terraced paddies, before she hits
the dusty road, stranded and stoned, wandering
by a sliver of moon.
He shakes her hard, as if the moon's stain would disappear.

Vāyu, God of Wind

All night you scrape at roof corrugations, churning river,
cloud or sky, turning a donkey's dreams to hysteria. Sleepless,
I ache, and think of trails your deer ride over the village.

How when Indra blows his flute he makes of you a *bhāvana*,
a *raag,* how *śruthi pavan* stirs if Sarasvatī plays her lute.
Govind teaches the *nada Brahmā* when Vishnu beats his drum.

By morning curtains dance, leaves are swept beneath my door.
The river bears the mark of your fingerprints, a thousand pieces
of wind carry away candles and marigolds from last night's *pūjā*.

In the temple of ears, you are daylight's voice, though we mortals
are never satisfied by your vibration, you, the bearer of Krishna's
semen. We cross valleys, *julas*, to arrive here, at *chakhra ananda*,

the heart centre, and in this breath I'm told, is *śabda Brahmā*,
the *ohm* or *aum*, a trinity, a diphthong. In naming a god,
our guttural, nasal, labial air lapses from sound into silence,

silence into trance. Govind teaches in Sanskrit, five *pranas*;
how the word *samana* means disturbance. He knows the colour
of the wind god, whose *vajra* is a weapon and a thunderbolt.

I watch the valley rinsed in light, the ashram windows tremble.
I feel a shiver in my wrist from my body's weight in *naga asana*,
and I think of Arjuna's long exile from the Pandavas in those hills

where sadhus roam, where the waterfalls, river caves and *tirthas*
still are; where the quiet, ancient India I have read about, still is.
And I am nothing but this breath. I am cloud, fern, smoke, moss.

The Stinking Mantra

I lay her under a camellia bush by the stone Buddha,
where a cherry blossom scattered its confetti karma,
where azaleas flourished and mynah birds convened.
Her pelt had been tattooed by a powerline. Night fell.
I almost forgot her because I was exhausted,
because I couldn't sleep, bypassing all attendant
thought of mourning. Outside the brushwood
stirred with native ghostings: her kind, not the shape
of hunger but death's apprentice slipping through trees,
their wire fingers scuffed against sky. The mist paused,
as if it were autumn, the trees were bare tightropes.
By daylight there were catkins, magpies broke the dawn,
the sky pinned back its rain, leaves were floating carp,
wisteria festooned desiccated gardens. I walked past lilies
with elephant ears swaying in the sun, a stop sign pulled
out from the ground by schoolboys. All this to slake me,
to dress my grief: these things with names to keep or to speak
as if articulation made of thought a substance.
Words, falling softly as feathers or pollen. How many words
might a woman discern? And what of a small marsupial
shocked by current, mid-climb, lit-up in free-fall?
What made me crush a blossom of wisteria to sprinkle
over the small, dead thing? Away I went to read the day's
diffuse paragraphs, to bluff my way through colouring-in,
a daughter's grammar. She ties toys with paperclip chains,
devices infinite to bind or to banish. Cars flew by,
a truck with a skip-bin, birds scavenged from the tarmac.
Up close, the possum smelt like rancid butter. I sat with
her and smoked, hearing nothing. No pity, no slight
for what I'd named her, *Sweet Shadow-Playing Funambulist.*

What was the harm? I might call her a crumpled stocking,
a ripple in the field, or a girl's dismembered evidence.
The swing tempts her back. Trucks pass rudely in the valley.
Soon her mouth began to fizz, filling with a residue
creamy as boot polish and everything pregnant with heat.
So the riddle of days, walking from doorstep to driveway
then back to school. *Disgusting*, my daughter said.
For at last the maggots came, teeming in the possum's
stopped, burned mouth. The air smelt of stewed semen,
the tongue like a black orchid, half-severed, dangled
and torqued. So the tongue swayed and in the fraying sleep
of my fatigue I could hear the quiet vowels, rising from
wisteria, from the hot ground, and falling back into silence.

Hymn

It is Spring; magnolia buds bloom,
the air seems to stretch and swell,
the plane trees are dappled like giraffe.

I am walking in a city without tanks
or curfews. In a city of loading zones
where the military is hardly visible.

The sky is moulded by impressions
of cumulus cloud, and that swallow
who skims across a streaky grey nimbus

looks like a hymn, disappearing behind
the garret of a half-demolished house,
a sparse block pending developers.

Why do I feel nervous about that hymn
as if all singing has been censored, since
I am not a relative of bird or cloud?

Why do I steal my fingers through the grass
whose rumours are haptic? They whisper
the wind's breath, the earth's furtive song.

The Mother, the Birds

And the birds fly out opening the sky's envelope
And the light almost violet is an amphitheatre.
And the homeward train is a calculus of memory.

The birds flow like water over quiet river stones,
And the light descends into a deepening velvet
To pillow the crescendo of a car's sound heard

When the child sleeps, when night is a window.
The iris of her writing is coloured in desire.
Evening is a stranger without reason or intuition.

A door shuts, a dinner plate signals the father,
Then dialogue stiffens, the sky's routine makes
All the feathers vanish, the page erase its birds.

The Mating Game

I, too, should like to clock my
long-distance blood. I'd like
to be tossed in high altitudes,

so foreign and far from home.
I'd curve my wings, I'd take
the advantage of a tailwind.

I'd follow frequencies unheard,
waves on distant shores, the sun
my compass, the canopies my grid.

But today the widowhood cock,
is released again. He's deprived
and unsatisfied, while his lesser

rival has a way with me. I'll search
the sky, imagine his quixotic race,
till he bows, coos at our dove-cote,

ever ardently. My own memory
of flight is swollen not by love
or grain, but by a hen's instinct.

Rainy Days

Glass beads of rain, melaleuca's fringe,
footsteps on the slippery timber boardwalk.

Children skipping puddles, her small hand
in mine as we walk to the classroom,

passing smiles from other mums: Chinese
Pakastani, Sikh. It's how the day begins

refreshingly, without poetry or poets,
the same constraints of time, and tolerance.

Could I bring back the guinea pig, she asks
in a cardboard box, for show-and-tell?

The trees are wet with a joy to remember,
ping-pong splashes, gumnuts, lichen freckles –

A yellow-veined plum blossom leaf
embossed against the car's windscreen.

River gutters float with crushed jacaranda,
Liesl and her Dutch mother ambling home.

Triptych of Wings

The air's thick with jasmine, agapanthus
lingering like incense in the still evening.
Today the monarch butterfly almost drowns
falling from leadlight to my daughter's bath
like Narcissus drawn to his shadow.

I watch him batter the glass incessantly,
in exhaustion caressing the window frame.
When I salvage him he stages death, wings
collapsing, legs folding neat as a parasol,
or a closing couplet, cleverly discreet.

We arrive in soft-blown jacaranda rain
to find the butterfly's choreography
outlived by lizards, rodents, a stray cat.
One wing is bright velvet, the other
Mendelian, a mosaic sequined with ants.

The Sculpture Garden

You enter the garden,
its fine mist, the exhibit
of a Japanese sculptor.
There's a walkway where broken timbers
give the illusion of neglect.
There in the pond among the weeds,
like tight bulbs of agapanthus
about to explode,
are Dadang Christanto's clay faces.
Their expressions replicate
astonishment, in different angles,
an enactment of war,
of death.

Leaving those expletives
you approach the bronze figure
of a woman's curves
in the dusty sunlight,
the body's question
too private for reply.
The posture arched,
the face not blemished
but ageing, like worry,
finely cracked.
Eyes closed, inverted hands
support the slender ache
of a half-moon.
Legs taut, her ribs could be
shelved with blank verse

so tidy, the syntax so wrought,
that it's dishonest.
It gets hard to breathe.

Do you hear
a soft hiss, whispering
of spine, bridge, hip
the unwritten trespasses?
The legs are restless. They quiver
as if Love itself walked through
this sculpture garden,
                                        leaving behind
an implausible want.

Pastiche

A winged hieroglyph, the ibis roams
into an architecture of cranes, gantry,
rows of terraces in their heritage tunics.

The park is littered with cigarette butts,
graffiti, the harbour is glazed;
a ferry chalks its way towards the pier.

Flags pole-dance in Woolloomooloo
where pedestrians gather for a drink
or a meal on a Friday evening in Spring.

I lie inertly on the grass, while another
foreigner, the Henry Moore statue,
inspires a different spatial boundary.

Later, driving north across the Bridge,
past the silver snake of a train, I try
to imagine a world without diversity.

Stalled in peak hour, I have time to consider
how greenhouse gases are choking the sky.
The parallax drift of roadworks, pylons,

jacaranda blooms are a montage, so familiar
that I feel carelessly numb, reading an sms
at the traffic lights, then texting back.

Circa 1916

Photograph by Paul Strand*

Who is this woman striding the sidewalk?
Swiftly departing the picture, a dowdy renegade
summoned from her errands by the clarinet player

on West 11th. So misaligned in the frame, as if
her gender's chained. Her hoops and haberdashery
are miniaturised by facades, their cubist shadows.

From the mirrored city, lips pressed, she elopes.
And her footprints scrape the day's inheritance.
Her incident abridged by the photographer's lens.

* *Paul Strand (1890–1976) was an American of Jewish descent. His photography of Wall Street is iconic for its psychological realism and formal abstraction.*

Kālī from Abroad

Kālī, you are the poster-goddess, sticking out your black
tongue, like Gene Simmons from Kiss, a kick in the teeth,
with your punk-blue leggings, your skull-and-scissor charms.

You swing a trident, a demon's head, and dance on the bones
of a pale Shiva. I recall the convincing eyes of a girl cripple
carrying your bottled effigy, as our bus careened to a dusty halt.

Some say you morphed from Pārvatī, drunk on blood,
others cite your superhero leap from Durgā's brow to slay
the self-cloning serpent before a Haka dance on mythic soil.

By a hundred Sanskrit names, India claims you in a single text,
while in *Zen and the Art of Motorcycle Maintenance*, you are
'the grass and the dew', on screen, our contemporary Judge Judy

having a bad hair day. I'd argue for your cosmopolitanism,
a global denizen, you're adroit in drugs and aphrodisiacs, a nude
dominatrix, a feminist export with a sadomasochistic bent.

A figure of partition you were cover girl for *Time* magazine.
A neo-pagan diva, your wholeness is darkness fashioned
from light, moon-breasted, with eyes of fire, with Brahma's feet,

Varuna's watery thighs. You rise from the grave, step over
carnage, feeding the world and your severed self with blood.
Stripped bare as Duchamp's Bride, you set bachelors in motion.

Pārvatī in Darlinghurst

So I lay on the body of a pale Shiva. He spoke
not a word, bothered perhaps by my nut-brown
skin, my slow dance calmed his electro shuffle.
A slap of limbs pinned him down to my earth.
I hadn't bathed in sandalwood, flouting legend
with a preference for Estée Lauder. The moon's
crescent tangled my hair, my breasts were bare,
our timing synchronised. Night fizzed, vanishing
into day, the club's hypnotic rhythms subdued.
We scorned the *Purānas*, our tryst no Himalayan
cave, but a hotel bed I had draped with stockings,
lingerie, and the crystal ice of a Third Eye. I admit
that's why I spoke with the speed of an antelope.
It seems the *acharyas* were mistaken: I hadn't
dated for marriage or adultery, nor with a wish
to deck his house with flowers or sweep his floors.
I am too busy, I declared, for dalliance or abstract
gossip. I have no interest in honeybees and birds.
All I wanted was a good time. I swear as the river
is my sister, that this guy was not my sun or my sky.
No way did it even enter my mind to have his kids.
His first wife's ashes are scattered all over the city.
Goddamn it, Shiva is a walking disaster; whatever
he touches burns. Restraining him with handcuffs
I said, 'Listen babe, your *lingam* and my *yoni* are
made for one thing only, improper and unchaste.
It's little more than conjecture to think our sweaty
helix could ever be whole.' Then I offered to grind
and gyrate him silly, suspend our want indefinitely,
and he fell utterly silent with this new meaning.

Durgā: a Self-Portrait

I see an icon of myself in the dark night of *amavasya*.
Mothers weep for young, married daughters, coming home.
They decorate my *pandal* with sweets, *paan* and *sindoor*.

I am saving my best argument against that feminine subject,
caught in another version of the dream. Here, the heat stifles
almost to inertia, the city shimmies with carnivalesque lights,

microphones, traffic horns, and one gaudy float after the next.
Sometimes I feel like a freak show, a cock in a frock, a new
machismo, lethal as Phoolan Devi or Buffy the Vampire Slayer,

though my preferred epithet is *Vindhayavasini*. I miss a terrain
of mountains where thunder shakes, where fog is a sky snake,
where monsoon slugs engorge to the size of Krishna's penis.

Today, I am androgynous, engineered as a split sex. I copy
Shiva's face, Vishnu's arms and Rama's hair. Light congeals
with strength in my bones to mend a crisis the male gods fail.

I memorise Mahisura's praise: *You are too beautiful for anything*
but love, he declares, *too delicate to fight*. Half an hour later, after
he morphs from a buffalo to an elephant, a lion to a man,

I castrate him with a graceful blow. My suitors surrender to this
transcendental play. And Vishnu, I spin him right round, like a record.
Men desire me for the fruit of knowledge. Want no handmaiden,

yet still a second sex; the sum of my parts being multiples of one.
My instruments, my weaponry and my props are channelled
from sensitive New Age gods, with their fondness for repetition.

She whose form is sleep, hunger, shadow or thirst, I'll wear
a virgin's blush. Tomorrow, I'll drink the blood of dacoits.
Send hail to the valley. Raze ten *lakh's* worth of rice and corn.

What I see is myself in this world: deviant, without genealogy.
Snow monkeys shiver in the deodar pines, goats loop in shelter.
Women abandon their duties, their grief, and Vishnu is paralysed.

The Dream Aesthetic of War

The suburbs are gridlocked
with school traffic.
I think of Beirut's collapsed ruins,
its clouds of black smoke.
How tuna hide nervously in the moorings
of deserted boats, the cats run feral,
how fruit ripens in unmanned stalls
of the bazaar.
And then I think of El-Baddhawi.
Orphans, checkpoints, over-crowded tents.
These scenes replayed like a drama,
a discourse, with its repetition
of consumption, interrogation.
We become agents of meaning
with our fetish of balance sheets,
transport, electronic mail.

At five o'clock we stretch our legs.
Take our silky terrier for a stroll.
Observe the sunset through antiquated trees
that weave along the sidewalk.
The pink and white camellia
deceptively homogenous,
like freshly coloured snow
in soft, slow decay,
each corolla rusting.
My daughter carefully
selects a handful for her craft.
Lately, I've watched her language deepen,
as though she's guessed a simile
might just preserve those petals.

While my mind petitions for an image
to make sense
of what it could signal
to be human in the First World.

I download blogs with bluetooth,
to tag the latest raid, Al-Quaeda style.
Watch news forbidden to my girl
who steals a momentary look
and boasts with alarming poise,
'Guess what, I've been watching the *bomb*!'
She's innocent of complexities,
words she can't pronounce:
Apache, Katyusha, Hezbollah.
Ever-seduced by language,
its mirror –
the image of an empty Shi'a mosque
resounding the muezzin's cry.

The Fire Eaters

Agni, did you come from lightning, sticky lava,
from dry, incendiary leaves or the sun's hot coals?

Long ago, in the middle Pleistocene, our fingers rubbed fire
our compact Homo sapien jaws ate warm flesh.

Worshippers, we stood up straight, to grip your spear.
How did we germinate these fields? Bonfires slaked you,

from the alchemy of brimstone and chalcedony sparks.
So temples shattered, so firearms and explosives broke

the great sleeping Buddhas of Ghandhara. We live in hope -
your seven tongues draw fire, deriving symbiotic flames

from air. Gums blister, lips kiss the burning world
goodbye, high on vapours, on singed skin and keratin.

The centuries drag. Our cartels breach the Orinocco,
the salt domes and Babylonian Mosques, unsympathetic

to prehistoric algae, the plankton time asphyxiates.
Tidy fossil beds are stripped, our pipelines carve

your thermal subjects. Nothing much survives: daughters
turn against fathers. Refineries melt, nuclear plants leak

apologetic isotopes. Yet, sunset converts our gestures
to atonement prepared from rice, cow dung, clarified ghee.

And somewhere with Promethean guile, a man wakes his lover
from her apartment as a light snow dusts the city streets.

In his arms, a two-litre soda bottle filled with gasoline,
on the landing, a dropped cigarette ignites your flint.

At West Head

There's nothing pure.
In this light, everything is polarised.
The sea spills dark letters,
a shifting alphabet.
We stand, half a shadow, on the beach.
Me, knowing that I'm still searching meaning
though I've stopped searching love.
Our solitude broken by a kookaburra,
a crow, a boy on the rocks
casting out a fishing line.
The sky is altered with methane
and everywhere signs of industry:
a rusted can of carpet cleaner,
a broken-lipped styrofoam cup,
an oil leak colouring the freshwater stream.
Nature's choked with similes.
Ant hills like pyramids,
a termite mound, the size of a helmet.
Death too, is artefact, a forgery traced
in this basket weave of leaf litter,
or the flowering banksia, shaved from its root.
Pink clouds meld into the horizon over Pittwater,
blending sky and sea in such seductive
haze that the headlands seem to be drifting
like all definitions.

Cowan Creek

Mudlapping, mud glitter, water shadows
shallow browns and green, the coarse sediment.
Oyster shells necklace the creek, its mangrove decay.
The rise and fall of the track teases us; there is
something wild beyond the brink of wealth, style, authority.
After the European cars, the sparkling marina, a diesel shift
freshens to cool heath. Stark ochre middens we pass,
with their tongues of First Nations, the sun's laser
diamond-pulse, avian arpeggios. In the canyon
it's so quiet you can hear the heart speak –
petulant, contradictory, famished.

Alchemy of Leaves

These mornings our hearts make a fist,
our dry throats shut.
Petals are stamped
to a violet pulp, as we sweep the park.
Eucalypt, gumnuts, oak,
strips of bark the wind ripped from tree trunks,
like dry flesh.
Nearby there's a street fair,
conversations float by.
Lovers saunter in the cool shade,
mothers trundle their strollers.
Fairy floss dissolves on children's tongues
as they skip home from the stalls
in the filigree shadows.
They head for the swing-set, the sandpit,
tiptoe past rose beds we've pruned,
waving balloons.
Sprinkles of pollen are a promise
we breathe.
Magnolia buds swell, rehearsing for rain.
I rake the lawn into small pillows of leaves.
There are clods, the soil fusty, sweet with decay.
I imagine the dampness of dew, rain, frost,
the tears we've shared
or concealed, at dusk.
The leaves are wrinkled, ragged
as the bruised wings of insects,
yet they tumble in wind-wheels.
A harmless percussion,
swept into decorum,
now the same dirt is caked under our nails.

Kissing Hamlet

A sparrow falls by providence, and the evening sky
is smeared indigo. I won't repeat our darling word
dusk, since breaking old habits is a new promise.
Sometimes the heart locks, before it dangles, ready
for releasing. Something in the amorphous shape
the trees espouse at this time of day is a resistance
to anything particular or complex, as if a more subtle
variation were possible. A toning down of contrast
makes the hour we named for us a kind of yielding.
We are something, you say, and I try to believe.
But even as I write the sky's streaks fade, the burls
of cloud formations begin to disappear, obeying
Newton's third law that for every act in this universe
there is an equal and opposite one. Today I walked
the streets, observing what I've missed of late –
a white magnolia in full bloom with delicately-scented
petals, chaste as Ophelia, among the topiary plants;
a house in ruins becoming some ugly new development.
And, of course, I thought of us – that hole we cut
in the stillness of evening, when the heart is disposed
to abandon the thought of never wanting this to stop.
The heart is mute but cries out in protest: 'Be free,
what are you afraid of?' Advice I tested last night
at the Opera Bar. I kissed the princely lips of madness:
Hamlet himself, after the proscenium. Not yet drunk.
His eyes, untamed, a little lost, perhaps. I trembled
but he didn't seem to mind, and I was glad, recalling
a soliloquy which speaks of fate's occasion being fickle,
how the end is ever present, how *the readiness is all*.
The harbour slapped softly, in Luna Park the Ferris wheel
turned. At least every so often, it is good to tremble.

And somehow the moment cured me of the incomplete metaphor of madness I had taken for myself. So moments change us, the evening bleeds and bruises. Words come to me as freely as a sparrow falls, unfastened by the sky.

José

The train passes the tranquil forest of Sils before Girona.
Afternoons are lethargic. A pestilence of flies, the sound of rifles.
'There's nothing here in this town', a German backpacker warns.

Unsure of the way, I sniff the piss along the quiet boulevarde.
They say the river has dried up, sprouting islands of weedy grass.
The pensione's owner is French but speaks *un poquito Ingles.*

There are mornings when I've woken to the rawness of the day,
to a city failing memory, as unforgiving as a lover, its fringes
blurring into chalky, yellow haze, its walls and citadels crumbling.

I want to remember the red earth, the white-washed village,
José playing guitar, the courtyard swirling as pigeon wings
shatter the Lorcan sky; his intricate flame, his *soléares.*

Amante de lo Ajeno

I'm framed between Doric pillars in dappled,
creamy light as peacocks strut. The photographer
from Figueres embeds a quiver in her camera.

After the cloisters hung with medieval tapestries,
dalmatics, chasubles of silver and gold brocade –
Who are you...and do you want to go for coffee?

Chocolat, churros y bouganvillea. The sky spits.
Tourists in the Jewish quarter turn their maps askew.
I can scarcely breathe for the caffeine, the scent of sex.

We stroll courtyards, garrisons. I run my hands
along the bevelled frame of a medieval casement,
try to guess the distant course a flying arrow takes,

only to be slaughtered by assassin eyes. Lipstick
stains, no other evidence. It's leafy-whispery dark
amid the ruins, a Moorish bath, and like a stranger's

curiosity, the bells of *la catedral* strike three times.
Nothing heroic to chase as the last ride leaves town.
Crazy boys I dodge speed uphill on motorbikes.

I pass tavernas, discos, drunken men who loiter in *ruas*.
Uncertain if it's me, a fragment, the precise moment
I'll cross the border to a turquoise lake, totems, frost,

the fading inflections. I rely on such desecrated things,
my passport creased, stamped, close to my skin. There's
a clamour in my throat, a small emergency of words.

After the Headlines

A city's candy lights are seen through cataracts.
At dusk, the quay shimmers, conceals its mystery.
Juanita, the dead model, suicides off The Gap
seem nothing in comparison to the ferry's claim.
After the news, I dreamt about the pleasure boat,
water gushing starboard, the sudden amputation,
a figure-skater's dress ballooning as she drowned
with a last pirouette to perfect her disappearance.
It wasn't a spectacle, or a Greek tragedy, but sad
to think of her body decomposing, a fine residue
of minerals for plankton and algae, for curious fish.
Days before there was a plane crash in Jogjakarta.
Award-winning journalists were burnt alive like fuel
for media barons and technophiles. It's strange
how we crave the visual, buying and selling images
of tsunamis, flash flooding, avian flu epidemics.
I heard patients in the waiting room speak about
this latest disaster, as if fate's occasion signalled
some compelling universal law that I should dread.
Sitting at my desk, I scanned the day's reports,
checking blood counts, electrolytes, cardiographs.
Whatever I've learnt in medicine, something slips
from the palanquin, refusing death, revived by more
than IV adrenaline, narcaine or shock can provide.
Like screen addicts we rehash the myths; the ultimate
getaway is a dream Corvette for our reticent ghosts.

Dying to Meet You

for Aravind Adiga

Maybe it wasn't deferred by the hardness of rain,
my lack of sincerity, your lover, an unfinished book,
a hangover; the cigarettes I didn't smoke to save
my lungs. I wasn't breathless last night. I dreamt
an email I opened from a publisher wishing me well
was an awful sign. You didn't even enter my dream,
though it would make poetic sense to mention loss
in imagined fragments: how I left my bangles by your
bedside table; how you asked me to slide them off
so they wouldn't chafe or ring the way memory does;
how you covered my pillowed face under a cold sheet.
I woke with a slight headache to morning's amnesia,
some days I know not who I am, or how to begin.
Yet, you're right. No one *is* dying to meet someone
like you. The poor are buried alive in seismic rubble,
their children swallowed by tsunamis are casualties
of global warming, overpopulation, urban sprawl.
How then to measure a grief which I sometimes desire
to share? How not to read your remarks as if you came
like an electronic prayer into my head? Is it worth you
knowing I trembled this morning at the very thought
of our real bodies meeting? Would I be grave? I am
so brittle lately, imperfectly divided. I am untouched.
In my yoga, you're not the Brahman from whom I draw
breath. Perhaps, by now, I might know the epic nature
of suffering; the way we can be prisoners and still free,
not by purchase or design. By readiness for what this
day brings do we exist in the spaces between words.

Reading The Mahābhārata

Once in a ruptured past before mutiny or *Midnight's Children*,
partition turning brother against brother, the Imperial tea-party
over, before the Monguls crossed the Ganges-Jumna doab,
or Tamberlane abandoned his jade and ribbed cantaloupe dome,

his leafy gardens of Samarkand, to turn infidels and polytheists
into a pyramid of skulls – the Rigveda was written as divine ink.
The sword proselytised; distinctions blurred between Hindu
and Muslim Sultans, forts of the Rajputs, their temples razed,

a hundred thousand slain by the Ghazis who looted rubies,
diamonds, garnets, tapestries of silver and gold brocade
in a measureless day. Before the syllables of Chinggis Khan's
army infused with the market vernacular into a new alphabet

rendering Urdu with its Nasta'liq calligraphy as the lingua franca,
idiom of poets, musicians, vocabulary of mosques, *mudrasahs*,
and today's Afghan refugees drifting homelessly through Pakistan,
an ancestral war distilled time's accretions, its battlefield dividing

myth and history. Dramatic tension follows when the stakes
are high. *Dharma, karma, moksha* are synonyms for one goal.
History accrues its errors as finite incidents, whereas like love,
myth endures. Filial and divine love was tested at Kurukshetra

between the Pāndavas and Kauravas, between Krishna and Kālī,
dynasties of gods and mortals. Arjuna's desire for Draupadi
matched by faultless archery in the *swayamwara*, was fraternally
coupled, a fated promise to his mother proving destiny is duty.

Sarasvatī, river of clemency, was a parched divan of cow dust.
As wisdom and nobility are fickle, Duryodhana fell into a pond
of his own reflection. Semi-divine, a father sightless, a mother
blindfolded by her compulsion to feel a husband's pain.

So the sons of darkness avenged their exemplary cousin
with loaded dice to bankrupt Yudhisthira, who gambled family
and kingdom. All five Pāndavas were exiled to other worlds,
Draupadi's honour was rescued, dressed by Krishna's seam.

These archetypes renewed in paintings, tabloid and screen were
first inscribed by Ganeśa, a hundred thousand verses, a frame-tale
of the Iron Age, which according to Pānini, the grammarian,
alludes to Romans, Huns and the Hellenistic floruit of Antioch.

Who were the Aryans? What men or gods? For what mad pursuit
did they abandon the oasis delta of Turkmenistan, its fire altars
and foal burials? What drove their *kafilas* beyond the Kabul valley,
the snows of the Hindu Kush towards the fertile plains of India?

Trade or climate change drove them south. Conquerors styled
on Indra himself, their wars and divisions are historicity, the subject
of a fossilised verse, which like the pottery of an ancient citadel
breathes life into an Indian heroic age, source of a timeless myth

whose elisions are perfect riddles, Attic shapes, truth's arithmetic.
For this, Ganeśa broke his tusk. Without pause or doubt Vyāsa spoke
his cosmic fiction synchronising Kālī's birth with the death of a god,
whose *vishvarūpa* form teases thought, slows time, all her silences.

Autumn

Wood smoke wafts in the performing eucalypts,
wind stirs in corridors around the sloping eaves.
Cicada nymphs have secretly buried their song.

Have you noticed the fragile scent of hyacinths?
How the heavily lacquered camellia, pink
reticulata and red japonica preserve their blush?

Indigo-grey, the colour of ghost gums slanting
into a faint sky is now compromised. The heart:
a lizard's pulsed inertia, no longer somersaults.

Maybe late afternoon is autumn; summer's retreat
not being archived, but suspended, as the feathered
vane of a bird wings its way across the avenue.

Meditations in the Canyon

You could walk for miles between sandstone walls or waterfalls
where the canyon is a womb, a wound

Carved out by wind which sweeps away bits of mallee, wattle,
buttongrass, my wasted thoughts.

Scarcely have I felt such a presence, we follow daylight's meridians,
invisible stars guide.

And we're fooled once more into taking all this for ourselves;
the ribboned trees, the secret stones.

Though the currawong does follow us a little of the way; he is
sharp-eyed, short necked.

I've seen spasm in a bird's flight: pinions flexed, a sleeve held
to her timorous breast.

Yet from here the view is pleasing: cliff shadows, light gauze
are worth the effort.

How I wish the birds would carry away my words, scatter them
into the bruised mouth of this gorge.

Sarasvatī's Scribe

I came in search of other gods:
the Vedic deities, the Mahadevis.
I found only a cripple
who limps along a narrow path,
lepers with hands like turnips.
Is this the form a god takes in the global village?
These children defecate
by the sacred river,
which flows into an archipelago of weeds.
The sweet smell of latrines suffuses
every bed I sleep in.
How sunlight is a blessing.
How the smell of shampoo,
or the fading cacophony
of tourist voices is bliss.
And if it really is Durga Puja,
where is her *wahan*?
Who would think her tiger's penis
is being used to treat impotence in China?
Perhaps I am mistaken, today, for Laksmī,
by the mother of a dehydrated infant
who begs a month's supply of NAN.
See, my hands have multiplied.
To germinate pink lotus flowers.
To empty out a currency in five-rupee coins.
How do I explain that I am not Laksmī,
but Sarasvatī's scribe searching
for a swan's slender neck, for the right words
to convince her that breastfeeding is safer
than imported milk
mixed with contaminated water.

Ganeśa Resurrected

What was it like to be dead? Not crucified or entombed,
whichever way you turned, your head sliced from your body
by Shiva's sword, while Parvati detoxed in a scented spa.

To be shaped from sandalwood by the hands of a goddess,
to invite the gesture of a *mudrā*, to be remodelled auspiciously
by a north-facing elephant, a *svástika*, a seal of the ancient Indus.

Lord of the *ganas*, a woman's dangerous moods returned your life,
improbable and half-remembered. You are not the father's phallus.
You guard the granaries, the terracotta tablets and inscriptions

of those cremated and uncremated. The heroes in temple carvings,
comic books, television dramas, and gold-foil Tanjore paintings
were recorded by you for Vyasa, the sage. What tectonic affair,

what orogeny hurtled you into the present? I wonder by what
Gangetic detour you arrived - Beas, Yamuna, Brahmaputra?
Perhaps your chakra is subterranean and your mantra a trinity.

Aum precedes afterlife: in one incarnation you are three worlds.
Your appellations translate appearance undecayed: a single tusk,
the fecundity of a potbelly and the feminine noun for wisdom.

I dreamed you came riding past my house on a skateboard.
Christ chose a donkey. But you, a spiritual pest inspector, arrived
to clean out the cobwebs, to expose the heart's furtive parasites.

There were rodents and menaces of all kinds I needed to subdue.
It was not by judgement, or prophecy, nor the visions of Ezekiel.
I had no wish to restore the dry bones - all I wanted was release.

You bridge the living gap between Brahmins and Sudras.
Congress pitched you, a symbol of protest against colonial rule –
god of everyman, everywoman, all sects. In the pantheon

of deities your rise is phenomenal. *Ganpati*, you're a celebrity
dancing in stone, wood or plaster. Acolyte or principal divinity,
you are a god of transitions, passages, doorways, merchants.

Once at Chaturthi, I saw you on a bright red *pandal* adorned
with vermillion, *kumkum* and *modakas*. Bhangra and hip-hop
played as you sunk beneath silt to where the river touches earth.

Enough

It is three am as I walk to the gate.
Dew glitters in the grass like fallen stars.
Naked trees are mannequins
dressing the street,
where yesterday's newspaper lies unread.
And on the corner the post box
waits for an old friend.
Even the sugar gliders are dormant.
The silence is vivid.
It burns like the red tip of a cigarette
from these numb fingers.
I think, perhaps, there's Venus in the sky's
phosphorescent waves.
Rain on the tarmac
is a white bird with a silver tail,
or a fish without eyes swimming
into my arms.
Last night my uncle's wife
died of a cancer
that hollowed out her bones.
I still have her locket in my dresser.
Speak no more of guilt for the lies
you leave behind,
for me.
Show me the disparity
between delight and pleasure,
if I should ask.
Tonight, it is enough
to walk no further than the gate.

Joy

The pink azaleas, their frosted mouths cry
open, as I take my evening stroll,
as the siren of an ambulance echoes
another rescue in the valley.
Strangers pass me in the dark,
like small gods, unannounced,
weary after the day's compromise.
This afternoon it rained bitterly.
Last night's snow was a cold blessing,
everywhere, so you said.
An email arrives twice,
like yesterday's headlines.
So much is uncertain.
Is anyone listening to these words?
Will the moon retract her promise
or elope?
Perhaps there is truth,
there are lies pretending to be truth.
There is someone falling hard,
and something falling out, carelessly
beautiful.
I would like to stop rehearsing.
I would like to love with an empty heart,
on days such as these, so swollen
with despair.
Somehow, I believe that you are mine.

The Piano Lesson

My hands are stricken. Do they not brush your sleeve?
Are they not stripped by this embrace? Such brevity:
light aslant on the maple, flooding us with its promise,
as if there were things outside our selves, or our words.

There are cities whose landscapes we chart. How dry
the river seems as dusk blanches. I twist in your arms,
where my aches and stings are electric. Your hammers
strike my strings, then rest, until the sound uncouples.

You have spent epistolary days rehearsing a solitary
composition; variations on the same étude to balance
what you have abandoned for loveliness. No exception
to this I fasten my bra as you lie, perfectly naked.

There's no indignity. I think we're saved by the purple
darkness. I return to the street, unable to disguise a flush
in my cheeks. Absorbed by stilettos, subways, the slow
traffic, for a few hours, I feel immortal as any fugitive.

What bitter chords should I wait for? I forget to ask.
You have tried to get behind all the music this world
makes. My hands are stricken by the lustre of ebony
at my keyboard. Now I work. Play the silent harmonics.

Two Souls

My cat cries when I enter the garden, as
if I have aroused her from winter's dream
or as if she wants to sing to me, her name.

What do cats dream of, Lord Krishna?
A coconut shell of milk or a glittering fish?
Now her slender limbs complete their asanas.

Now her neck arches, her jaw, an elastic.
The sharp eye constricts, discerns wind
in the quivering grass from a grasshopper's

camouflage. But there's no mistaking Maya.
My cat rehearses the accurate lunge of her paw.
She cries as one compelled, hungry, yet not.

Perhaps my being here deserves an answer.
For weeks I too have watched her, how
she hunts. I've heard the moan of her catch

at dusk, which is your hour, Lord Krishna.
Then, no bird sings and only a cat with two souls
dreams of death, her stigma left on a lizard

or on a butterfly, whatever moves towards
the shadow of meaning. As I am born of fire
I burn, my Lord, but I sleep in your arms.

I am one Upanishad moon on fragrant nights.
By day I am the consort of oceans, rice fields,
pale and invisible to you as the sky's temple.

Laksmī under Oath

I left my footprints on the threshold
of ancient temples, pointing
inwards, like the flow of fortune.

In 200 BC, well-intentioned seers
fashioned me, etched in bronze
on lintels, the gateways to the city.

The land was barren, a salt marsh
where Indra slayed a three-headed fiend,
pole stars drifting and rivers forked.

How my parasitic limbs ached,
my breast cut off, its vestiges leaking
milk. I was spared of Vedic hymns,

a self-sovereign. The villagers
offered testimony in ricecakes, garlands,
jhoti. Untouchables defiled me.

Brahmin beggars stalked me, carping
for centuries. From that sensual debut
I was glitter in the ocean's foam.

Here are my breasts, and here
are my twenty acrylic nails, my spinal
brace, my club feet and pressure sores.

All this lotus mania! Crouching in Ganges
mud takes its toll. Even poets are stalking me.
I am dripping in gold, they can't resist.

Close-up, the room is full of strangers,
shaking, coughing, as I sign the affidavit
(in my red half-slip) and swallow a pill.

Vishnu, I am not bipolar, I am post-op,
with a restylane flush, on a spending spree,
unfolding in you, as the moon would.

Indra's Net

I have not found your idol in any temple, Lord.
Your one thousand eyes elude me in sleep, your
net of pearls shimmering like pins, a flower sutra.

Yet, how the Vedic skies praise your light.
Spear fisherman and hunter, each knot you tie
interweaving memory, a reef with a rosebud.

Bowlines and clove hitches are your fetters, all
the lace and twine of this world, the emptiness
it frames, uncharted. Your past might be a silk road

of gold, hemp, musk, caravans loaded with spice,
slaves traded. In my conjuring there are far colonies,
papyrus treaties, gold coins, pierced and printed

with your cognate deities: Thor of old Norse, Zeus,
whose thunder you whet, Bacchus, the soma-drinking
foreigner. Zoroastrian or Armenian, your polyglot

perplexes linguists with a strange loop of origin.
Like Escher's *Drawing Hands* you are a paradox
to muzzle me. Water nymphs grace your cloud court,

a half-horse, a man with a bird's wing, his fibula
inscribed with runes. Even the jade and dewpond
are small miracles, selfless things inventing selves.

Somewhere, a River

Before the light's particle rays pencil to floating
leaves, fingerlings, I've left him in a sea of sheets,
his dreaming, a cold waste. Abrasive snores drift
through snow blankets, underwater eyes unseen.

Deep to the surface a totemic legend rudders past
my coracle. I rest in wood rot, salt licking the skin
of my thigh. The scoop hem of a silk nightdress
with its black trimming ties, flutters in the breeze.

Here a lamprey eel's stone mouth gapes in frigid
holes the ice composes like a riddle. A new moon
spares the sky's spectacle, intuitively reticent, or
maybe hardened by frost stars setting fire to the hills.

Birds begin to trill their silent score for late dreams.
The boat leaks, cloud water drawn in sapphire amulets
to wrap my limbs. Morning will sprinkle the conifers,
illumine map or dictionary, if not the treaty concealed

by my tarpaulin. I'd like to seed in a grave of mink,
Tuchone, buffalo bones, or in a deep nest where
sleeping fish wait to spawn. When the rapids come
and the wild crocus shoots, the inconnu will abandon.

For now, I am frozen, somewhere between aquatic
and terrestrial. I guess the river's arctic bend, imagine
nautical light, reading the smoke. Let wildfires reach,
groundwater springs rise; deadly, the snow melting.

The Spirit House

By whose hand is the evening
painted in stillness?

Dark pillow of clouds beneath
which swallows are frenetic.

Sunset is a smear of mauve-
gold, of drums and motorbikes.

At this hour, the temple
pagodas are carved silhouettes,

our thoughts are framed by arbors.
Sandat and frangipani scarcely

beg the sky's empty bowl.
Ducks reel in the glittering rice.

The leaves are enamelled, after rain,
our words have no echoes.

Why do I doubt that hungry gods
prey upon the butterflies' dance?

Tonight, I heard a god's orgasm
turn to stone by the spirit house.

Notes

With some modifications, I have chosen to use the International Alphabet of Sanskrit Transliteration (IAST) standards with diacritics for romanising Sanskrit references in this book. This is a reminder of differences between English and Devangari phonetics.

To acknowledge the syncretism of languages the following notes accompany individual poems, citing references as well as translations where appropriate.

Vishvarūpa

Sanskrit meaning: manifold, having all forms and colours.

Vishvarūpa was the divine revelation by Krishna to Aravanan in the Bhagavad Gīta.

Deva Loka

deva loka: place of the gods

mukti: liberation, being devoid of body

nāmarūpa: corporeality, name and form, rupa referring to the representation of the Gods.

tribhanga: tri-bent posture found in Indian art, sculpture and classical dance. Compared to contrapposto, this stance is more sensual as it consists in bending the neck, waist and knee.

chanda: a wish, a wholesome desire. Chanda is also the goddess Devi.

gopi: milkmaid, they are also the mythological companions of Krishna.

sal: a type of tree found in the forests of Himachal Pradesh, considered to be holy by Hindus and Buddhists. Some scriptures describe the Buddha being born and dying under the sal.

bhojpatra: a Himalayan birch, its bark was used for writing in ancient times.

Ode to Mumbai

jaggery: a sweet sugar, made of cane

bailadeira: Portuguese for 'dancing girl', this was a common description for the devadasis of temples in Oriental colonial literatures.

hijra: eunuch or transvestite

Prayerflags from Dharamsala

Dussehra: a popular festival, which celebrates Durgā's victory and worship.

Lung-ta: a horizontal Tibetan prayer flag, meaning the Windhorse.

rangzen: freedom

fakir: beggar

Six Myths of Love

Asclepios: a medical doctor in Greek mythology

City of Another Home

jīva: soul

pomfret: butterfish, from the Portuguese, pambo, a local delicacy

kolambi: prawn rice

pūjā: prayer, honour, worship

gymkhana: an Anglo-Indian word derives from the Hindi word for racket sports, and refers to a gymnasium

wallah: Hindi suffix indicating a person involved in some labour or activity.

Sīta

An avatar of Laksmī, and the wife of Rāma, one of the principal characters in the Rāmāyana, she faced adversity, was kidnapped, and is said to embody womanly virtues. Hindu transsexuals and transvestites identify with her suffering.

kothi: homosexual male

dalit: untouchable

bhangi: sweeper caste

dhobi: a caste who specialise as launderers, they wash clothes in rivers and sea ghats

chawl: a building of 4–5 storeys, tenements for the middle class

ghagra: skirt

Mohini: Lord Krishna assumes the form of a beautiful woman Mohini who agrees to marry Aravanan, destined to be sacrificed to the goddess Kālī. Hijras in India identify with Mohini.

Hanumān

Hanumān is the monkey god; half man, half monkey

pushpa: flowers

chandan: sandalwood

deepak: scent used for sacred lamps

dhoop: a concentrated incense

paan: betel leaf and areca nut chewed for its palate freshening and relaxant properties

yojanas: a Vedic measure of distance used in ancient India. The exact measurement is disputed amongst scholars with distances being given between 6 to 15 kilometers.

Shaping the Linga

Shiva is thought to be derived from the god Rudra who dates to the Rigveda: 1700–1100 BC.

This poem references the Goan Inquisition by the Portuguese colonists who forced mass conversions of Hindus to Christianity.

Shivalinga: is a phallic icon of worship of the god Shiva found in South Asia. It may be made of stone, wood or ghee (butter).

mahadevas: female goddesses

kalavant: temple-dwelling musicians, many of whom under the religious intolerance of Portuguese rule fled to Bombay.

Vāyu, God of Wind

bhāvana: a calling into being

raag: a sung prayer

śruthi pavan: the smallest interval of pitch, of the wind god *nada Brahmā*: song of God

pūjā: prayer, honour, worship

julas: bridges

chakra ananda: the heart chakra

śabda Brahmā: sound of God

naga asana: a yoga posture, know as the cobra

Kālī from Abroad

Kālī derives from the word kāla, which means black, time, death. Her worship dates from 600 AD.

This poem is inspired by Octavio Paz's essay on the art of Marcel Duchamp, 'The Castle of Purity', from Marcel Duchamp, *Appearance Stripped Bare* (Arcade, New York, 1990), pp. 64–69.

Zen and the Art of Motorcyle Maintenance, by Robert M. Pirsig (William Morrow, 1974) quoted reference to Kali, p. 329.

Pārvatī in Darlinghurst

The idea that the great male gods all possess an inherent power through which they undertake creative activity is assumed in Hindu philosophical thought. When this power, or Shakti, is personified, it is always in the form of a goddess. Pārvatī assumes the identity of Shiva's Shakti. In this active, creative role she is identified with *prakrti* (nature, creative force), whereas Shiva is identified with *purusha* (pure spirit). This poem re-reads the stereotyping of these iconic images.

Purāna: Hindu, Jain and Buddhist religious texts told as narratives of the universe, its creation and destruction.

acharyas (ācārya): religious guides or teachers

lingam: meaning mark or sign, considered a symbol of the phallus.

yoni: refers to the female genitalia, also it may refer to a source, space, divine passage, sacred temple, spring, fountain.

Durgā: a Self Portrait

amāvāsya: the new moon

paan: betel leaf and areca nut chewed for its palate freshening and relaxant properties

sindoor: vermilion, which comes from the powdered mineral cinnabar

Phoolan Devi: The Bandit Queen, a notorious Dalit outlaw believed she was a reincarnation of Durgā

Vindhayavasini: an epithet for Durgā, meaning she who dwells in the Vindya mountains

Reading the Mahābhārata

madrasahs: schools for the teaching of Islam

dharma: duty

karma: pleasure, aesthetic experience

moksha: liberation

swayamwara: ritual practice of chosing a husband. In the case of Draupadi suitors had to hit a fish's eye with their arrow. This fish was an image rotating on a wheel, placed in a pan filled with water.

Pānini: an ancient Sanskrit linguist and grammarian

kafilas: camel caravans

Sarasvatī's Scribe

Sarasvatī is the goddess of the arts and knowledge. Her *wahan*, or vehicle, is a swan.

Laksmī is the goddess of wealth and good fortune.

Durgā is a goddess of a thousand arms.

Durga Puja is an important festival in the Hindu calendar.

Ganeśa Resurrected

Ganeśa or Ganesh emerged as a deity in the 4–5 C BC. He is widely worshipped among many sects; he is the remover of obstacles and the deva of intellect and wisdom, the child of Shiva and Pārvatī.

svastika: a crossing of the arms, an auspicious object. In its clockwise direction this ancient Sanskrit symbol represents Ganesh.

mudrās: hand gestures used to depict the deities and in traditional dance.

Vyāsa: the sage said to be the author of the Mahābhārata, Ganesh its scribe.

Aum Ganeśa is identified with the Hindu mantra Om, the trinity of fire, air, sun. He embodies the primal sound.

chakra: according to Kundalini yoga Ganeśa is said to reside in the base or foundation chakra, *Mūlādhāra*.

pandal: platform

kumkum: coloured powder made from turmeric, saffron and slaked lime, often marked between the eyes over the sixth chakra, or third eye.

modaka: sweets offered

Chaturthi: an annual festival for Ganesh when his murtis are immersed in water.

Two Souls

Krishna emerged as a deity around 400 BC.

This poem references the Hindu Vedic philosophy of non-dualism, where there is no separation between the soul and Brahma. Krishna teaches there are two paths to this state: that of action and that of contemplation.

Maya is the world of the senses and of ignorance.

Laksmī under Oath

Goddess Laksmī: she is the female counterpart of the supreme being and wife of Vishnu.

laksmī: means wealth, good fortune, wife of a hero.

jhoti: intricate decorations traced in rice flour paste on the walls and floors.

Laksmi Tata was an Indian girl born as a conjoined twin to poor labourers in 2005 in the state of Bihar. She was named after the goddess of wealth. She underwent extensive multi-operator surgery and remains disabled and in need of further surgery. She was thought to be a gift from the goddess.

Indra's Net

Indra's net connotes the interrelatedness of all appearances as being reflections of others. It encompasses the notion of non-self.

The god Indra is related to other Indo-European gods: Thor, Peron, Zeus and Dionysus. His origins may connect to Indara worshipped in northern Syria circa 1500 BC. He is the god of storms, rain, war.

The metaphor of Indra's net was developed by the Mahayana Buddhist school in the third century scriptures of the Avatamsaka Sutra.

The Spirit House

sandat: a Balinese flower used in offerings to the gods.

Acknowledgements

Poems from this collection have appeared in the following journals and collections.

Antipodes (USA), *Asia Literary Review* (Hong Kong), *Australian Literary Review*, *Blue Dog*, *Cordite*, *Crannóg Magazine* (Ireland), *Drunken Boat* (USA), *Etchings*, *Fox Chase Review* (USA), *HEAT*, *Indian Literature* (India), *Island*, *Joao-Roque Literary Journal*, *Journal of The Poetry Society of India*, *Lemuria* (India), *Mascara Literary Review*, *Meanjin*, *Muse India*, *nzepz*, *Overland*, *Philament*, *Pennsylvania Literary Journal* (USA), *Poetry Ireland Review* (Ireland), *Poetry Macao*, *Prosopisia* (India), *Quarterly Literary Review Singapore*, *Quill* (Malaysia), *Red Leaves*, *Seva Bharati Journal of English Studies* (India), *Softblow* (Singapore), *Southerly*, *The Age*, *The Sun Herald*, *Thylazine*, *Wet Ink*, *World Literature Today* (USA), *Writers' Hub* (UK).

Not A Muse (Haven, Hong Kong, 2009), *The 2008 Newcastle Poetry Prize Anthology*, *The Best Australian Poems 2009* (ed. Robert Adamson, Black Inc.), *The HarperCollins Book of Modern English Poetry by Indians* (ed. Sudeep Sen, HarperCollins, 2011), *Another English: Anglophone Poets from Around the World* (eds Catherine Barnett and Tiphanie Yanique, Tupelo, USA, 2014).

This manuscript was completed with the assistance of a Professional Development Grant from the Copyright Agency Limited and a Poetry Mentorship awarded by the Australian Society of Authors in 2008.

My heartfelt thanks to Judith Beveridge for her friendship and for mentoring me in writing these poems.

I would like also to thank friends and colleagues Jo Langdon, Lindsay Tuggle, Anne Walsh, Tamryn Bennett, Keki Daruwalla, Sudeep Sen, Jenny Lewis, Nicholas Jose, Terri-ann White and Anne Brewster. Special thanks to Kelly Somers, Eleanor Hurt and Kate Pickard from UWA Publishing.